4142 .N43 2003

ale, Thomas H.

eechwriting in perspective

WITHDRAWN

Parkland College Library
2400 West Bradley Avenue
Champaign, IL 61821

SPEECHWRITING IN PERSPECTIVE

SPEECHWRITING IN PERSPECTIVE

THOMAS H. NEALE
AND
JEAN M. BOWERS

Novinka Books
New York

Senior Editors: Susan Boriotti and Donna Dennis
Coordinating Editor: Tatiana Shohov
Office Manager: Annette Hellinger
Graphics: Wanda Serrano
Editorial Production: Maya Colmbus, Alexis Klestov, Vladimir Klestov,
Matthew Kozlowski and Lorna Loperfido
Circulation: Ave Maria Gonzalez, Vera Popovic, Raymond Davis, Melissa Diaz,
Magdalena Nuñez, Marlene Nuñez and Jeannie Pappas
Communications and Acquisitions: Serge P. Shohov
Marketing: Cathy DeGregory

Library of Congress Cataloging-in-Publication Data
Available Upon Request

ISBN: 1-59033-606-2.

Copyright © 2003 by Novinka Books, An Imprint of
Nova Science Publishers, Inc.
400 Oser Ave, Suite 1600
Hauppauge, New York 11788-3619
Tele. 631-231-7269   Fax 631-231-8175
e-mail: Novascience@earthlink.net
Web Site: http://www.novapublishers.com

All rights reserved. No part of this book may be reproduced, stored in a retrieval system or transmitted in any form or by any means: electronic, electrostatic, magnetic, tape, mechanical photocopying, recording or otherwise without permission from the publishers.

The publisher has taken reasonable care in the preparation of this book, but makes no expressed or implied warranty of any kind and assumes no responsibility for any errors or omissions. No liability is assumed for incidental or consequential damages in connection with or arising out of information contained in this book. Any parts of this book based on government reports are so indicated and copyright is claimed for those parts to the extent applicable to compilations of such works.

This publication is designed to provide accurate and authoritative information with regard to the subject matter covered herein. It is sold with the clear understanding that the publisher is not engaged in rendering legal or any other professional services. If legal or any other expert assistance is required, the services of a competent person should be sought. FROM A DECLARATION OF PARTICIPANTS JOINTLY ADOPTED BY A COMMITTEE OF THE AMERICAN BAR ASSOCIATION AND A COMMITTEE OF PUBLISHERS.

29.50

Printed in the United States of America

Contents

Preface vii

Chapter 1 Public Speaking and Speechwriting:
Selected References 1
Jean M. Bowers

Chapter 2 Speechwriting in Perspective: A Brief Guide
to Effective and Persuasive Communication 11
Thomas H. Neale

Index 37

PREFACE

The first chapter is a bibliography which lists books and articles that offer advice on the presentation of a speech and provide materials from which to develop a speech. It includes how-to manuals, examples and critiques of great speeches, and anthologies of quotations and humorous stories for use in speechwriting. The last section is a listing of materials prepared by CRS which might help to prepare the speaker for specific occasions and holidays.

Chapter two provides basic guidance on obtaining speech material, using it to prepare a speech draft, and presentation.

Chapter 1

PUBLIC SPEAKING AND SPEECHWRITING: SELECTED REFERENCES

Jean M. Bowers

INTRODUCTION

This bibliography lists books and articles which offer advice on the presentation of a speech and provide materials from which to develop a speech. It includes how-to manuals, examples and critiques of great speeches, and anthologies of quotations and humorous stories for use in speechwriting. The last section is a listing of materials prepared by CRS which might help to prepare the speaker for specific occasions and holidays.

Books listed are selected from the Library of Congress Computerized files and a few articles have been selected from the CRS Public Policy Literature file. Congressional staff may request copies of items listed by calling 5-5700 or FAX (7-6745). Because of limited photocopy resources, please limit items requested to 10. Other users should contact a local public or university library.

PUBLIC SPEAKING: METHOD

Axon, David E. Stine, Richard L. The public speaking process: computer-assisted speech organization and development. Fort Worth, Harcourt Brace Jovanovich College Publishers, 1993. 381 p. PN4121.A85 1993.

Ayres, Joe. Miller, Janice. Effective public speaking. Madison, Wis. W.C. Brown, 1994. 349 p. PN4121.A9 1994.

Blake, Cecil A. Public speaking: a twenty-first century perspective. Dubuque, Iowa, Kendall/Hunt, 1995. 346 p. PN4121.B525 1995.

Bordeaux, Jean. Allen, Roberta. How to talk more effectively. [Chicago] American School, 1993. 239 p. PN4121.B545 1993.

Boyd, Kathy. Accept no limitations. Glendora, CA, Royal Pub., 347 p. 1995. PN4121.A34 1995.

Breaden, Barbara L. Speaking to persuade. Fort Worth, TX, Harcourt Brace College, 1996. 274 p. PN4181.B695 1996.

Carlile, Clark Stites. 38 basic speech experiences. Topeka, Kan., Clark Pub., 1993. 218 p. PN4121.C24 1993.

DeVito, Joseph A. The elements of public speaking. New York, Longman, 1997. 486 p. PN4121.D389 1997.

Hamilton, Cheryl. Successful public speaking. Belmont, Wadsworth Pub. Co., 1996. 432 p. PN4121.H19 1996. Includes section on persuasive speaking.

Harlan, Ray. The confident speaker: how to master fear and persuade an audience. Bradenton, Fla., McGuinn & McGuire Pub., 1993. 274 p. PN4121.H262 1993.

Hasling, John. The audience, the message, the speaker. New York, McGraw-Hill, 1993. 224 p. PN4121.H267 1993.

Hilton, Jack C. How to meet the press: a survival guide. Champaign, Ill., Sagamore Pub., 1990. 200 p. PN4193.P73H54 1990.

How to become an effective speaker. Ramsey, N.J., Alexander Hamilton Institute, 1995. 208 p. PN4121.H588 1995.

Humes, James C. The Sir Winston method: the five secrets of speaking the language of leadership. New York, Quill/William Morrow, 1993. 189 p. PN4121.H858 1993.

Kearney, Patricia. Public speaking in a diverse society. Mountain View, Calif, Mayfield Pub. Co., 1996. 481 p. PN4121.K3375 1996.

Klepper, Michael M. I'd rather die than give a speech. Secaucus, N.J., Carol Pub. Group, 1995. 177 p. PN4121.K662 1995.

Maloney, Stephen R. Speaker's portable answer book. Englewood Cliffs, N.J., Prentice Hall, 1993. 292 p. PN4121.M3185 1993.

Metcalfe, Sheldon. Building a speech. Fort Worth, Tex., Harcourt Press, 1994. 484 p. PN4121.M5525 1994.

Milton, Hal. Going public: a practical guide to developing personal charisma. Deerfield Beach, Fla. Health Communications, 1995. 147 p. Public speaking; acting. PN4121.M5625 1995.

Mira, Thomas K. Speak now, or forever fall to pieces. 1st ed. New York, Random House, 1995. 161 p. PN4121.M5655 1955.

Nadeau, Ray E. Speaking effectively in public settings: a modern rhetoric with a traditional base. Lanham, Md., University Press of America, 1993. 277 p. PN4121.N243 1993.

Payne, James. Carlin, Diana Prentice. Getting started in public speaking. Lincolnwood, Ill., National Textbook Co., 1994. 128 p. PN4121.P317 1994.

Pearce, Terry. Leading out loud: the authentic speaker, the credible leader. 1st ed. San Francisco; Jossey-Bass Publishers, 1995. 174 p. HD57.7.P4 1995.

Powers, John H. Public speaking: the lively art. New York, Harper Collins College Publishers, 1994. 455 p. PN4121.P647 1994.

Roan, Carol. Speak easy: a guide to successful performances, presentations, speeches, and lectures. Washington, D.C. Starrhill Press, 1995. 96 p. PN4121.R58 1995.

Schriner, Brian. Public speaking: a traditional approach in a modern world. Needham Heights, MA. Simon & Schuster Custom Pub., 1996. 247 p. PN4121.S2866 1996.

The Speech: a guide to effective speaking. By the faculty in effective speaking at Cazenovia College. Dubuque, Iowa, Kendall/Hunt, 1993. 84 p. PN4121.S752 1993.

Sprague, Jo. The speaker's handbook. 4th ed. Fort Worth, Harcourt Brace, 1996. 457 p. PN4121.S777 1996.

Successful speech. Edited by Michelle Bailey, Ted Scutti and Frank Irizarry. Taos, NM, CDE, 1995. 261 p. PN4121.S8346 1996. Compilation of essays by speech educators.

Thorek, Philip. Open your mouth but don't say "ah!": RX for public speaking. New York, Igaku-Shoin, 1994. 70 p. PN4121.T535 1994.

Verderber, Rudolph F. The challenge of effective speaking. Belmont, Calif., Wadsworth Pub. Co., 1997. 488 p. PN4121.V4 1997.

Walters, Lillet. Secrets of successful speakers: how you can motivate, captivate, and persuade. New York, McGraw-Hill, 1993. 216 p. PN4121.W327 1993.

Wilder, Claudyne. The presentations kit: 10 steps for selling your ideas. New York, Wiley, 1994. 294 p. PN4121.W386 1994.

Wolvin, Andrew D. The public speaker, the public listener. Boston, Houghton Mifflin Co., 1993. 300 p. PN4121.W535 1993.

Zarefsky, David. Public speaking: strategies for success. Needham Heights, MA, Allyn and Bacon, 1996. 511 p. PN4121.Z37 1996. Author is a professor at Northwestern University.

SPEECHWRITING

Method

Cook, Jeff Scott. The elements of speechwriting and public speaking. New York, Collier Books, 1991. 242 p. PN4142.C66 1991.

Dance, Frank E.X. Speaking your mind: private thinking and public speaking. 2nd ed. Dubuque, Iowa, Kendall/Hunt, 1996. 356 p. PN4121.D336 1996. Speech preparation and delivery.

Detz, Joan. How to write and give a speech: a practical guide for executives, PR people, managers, fund-raisers, politicians, educators, and anyone who has to make every word count. New York, St. Martin's Press, 1992. 204 p. PN4121.D388 1992.

Ehrlich, Henry. Writing effective speeches. New York, Paragon House, 1992. 214 p. PN4142.E37 1992.

Germer, Fawn. Are quotes sacred? American journalism review, v. 17, Sept. 1995: 34-37. LRS95-8480. "Some journalists say it's fine to 'improve' quotations as long as the meaning isn't changed. Others argue that the practice is dishonest."

Gilman, Andrew. Get to the point: how to say what you mean and get what you want. Dubuque, Iowa, Kendall/Hunt, 1995. 244 p. PN4121.G4585 1995. Message suggestions and speech delivery.

Gotschall, Mary G. The lost art of speechmaking. Campaigns & elections, v. 14, June-July 1993: 48-49. LRS93-4855. "Four veteran wordsmiths reveal the secrets of writing and delivering effective speeches."

Merrill, Norman W. Who was that woman I didn't see you with last night? New England journal of public policy, v. 6, fall-winter 1990: 61-76. LRS90-11666. Presents a short history of negative campaigning in America.

Miller, N. Edd. Boyd, Stephen. Public speaking: a practical handbook. Bloomington Ind., Tichenor Pub. Group, 1989. 148 p. PN4121.M5568 1989.

Minnick, Dale L. Speaking without fear. Woodward, OK, 1995. 196 p. PN4121.M56287 1995. Speechwriting and delivery.

Outzs, Lori L. A principled use of congressional floor speeches in statutory interpretation. Columbia journal of law and social problems, v. 28, winter 1995: 297-338. LRS95-2700. Comment "suggests that floor statements, which are crucial pieces of legislative history for federal statutes, be used in a principled manner that analyzes the role of the statement's speaker and the context of the statement. The Author demonstrates this interpretational method through a review of the opinions of Justices Brennan and Rehnquist in United Steelworkers of America v. Weber. The Author recommends... that the Congress amend its record-keeping procedures to facilitate this usage."

Pendleton, Winston K. Speaker's handbook of successful openers and closers. Englewood Cliffs, N.J., Prentice-Hall, 1984. 261 p. PN4193.I5P44 1984. Samples of opening and closing statements.

Political images. State government news, v. 36, July 1993: 15-29. LRS93-6449. Contents: The positive side of negative advertising: campaigns can be won by exposing an opponent's weak points, by Greg Stevens; Swiss cheese journalism: the outlook is bleak for expanding statehouse coverage, by Doris A. Graber; Doubts about doublespeak: confusion, not communication, is the point of this art, by William Lutz; Statehouse news: how to turn the media's attention to issues of substance, by David Yepsen; Mixed messages: the language of politics is not all that it appears, by Julie C. Olberding.

Rackleff, Robert B. The art of speech writing. Vital speeches of the day, v. 54, Mar. 1, 1988: 311-314. LRS88-15546. A speech on the steps to writing a good speech.

Sellers, Jim. Speeches that leave them speechless. State government news, v. 37, no. 6, June 1994: 11-14. LRS94-5786. "A great speech appeals to your imagination as well as your ear."

Strother, David B. The quality of expression: a guide to practical criticism. Dubuque, Iowa, Kendall/Hunt Pub. Co., 1990. 104 p. PN4121.S8328 1990.

University of Kansas. Communication Studies Dept. Virtual presentation assistant [online] (as of Dec. 5, 1996). Available internet: http://www.ukans.edu/cwis/units/coms2/vpa/vpa.htm. LRS96-7948. Contents: Determining your purpose; Selecting your topic; Researching your topic; Analyzing your audience; Supporting your points; Outlining your points; Using visual aids; Presenting your speech. Reference material on the Internet for which CRS is providing an address only.

Research

Famous Speakers and Speeches: Text and Analyses
American orators before 1900: critical studies and sources. Edited by Bernard K. Duffy and Halford R. Ryan. New York, Greenwood Press, 1987. 481 p. PN4055.U5A4 1987.

American public discourse: a multicultural perspective. Lanham, Md., University Press of America, 1992. 328 p. E184.A1A6365 1992. Includes speeches by Native American females, males, African American females and males, Mexican American females and males and White American females.

Bochin, Hal. Richard Nixon: rhetorical stategist. New York, Greenwood Press, 1990. 223 p. E856.B58 1990.

Braude, Jacob Morton. Complete speaker's and toastmaster's library. Englewood Cliffs, N.J., Prentice Hall, 1992. PN4121.B68 1992. Speech material by subject.

Contemporary American public discourse: a collection of speeches and critical essays by Halford Ross Ryan. Prospect Heights, Ill., Waveland Press, 1992. 384 p. PS668.C58 1992.

Fleser, Arthur F. A rhetorical study of the speaking of Calvin Coolidge. Lewistown, N.Y., E. Mellen Press, 1990. 118 p. E792.F54 1990.

Friedenberg, Robert V. Theodore Roosevelt and the rhetoric of militant decency. New York, Greenwood Press, 1990. 209 p. E757.F84 1990. Theodore Roosevelt: presidential messages.

Gelderman, Carol. All the Presidents' words. Wilson quarterly, v. 19, spring 1995: 68-79. LRS95-3775.

Goldzwig, Steven R. Dionisopoulos, George N. In a perilous hour: the public address of John F. Kennedy. Westport, Conn., Greenwood Press, 1995. 219 p. E842.1.G65 1995.

The Great American priorities. Edited by George L. Berg, Jr. Lanham, Md., University Press of America, 1992. 364 p. E839.5.G74 1992. Collects "speeches on a variety of subjects, ranging from agriculture to refugees, and from youth to patriotism."

Great American speeches. Edited, with introduction by Gregory R. Suriano. New York, Gramercy Books, 1993. 308 p. E183.G68 1993.

Great speeches for criticism and analysis. Selected by Lloyd E. Rohler and Roger Cook. Greenwood, Ind., Alister Press, 1988. 336 p. PS668.G74 1988. Kinds of speeches included: campaign, rally, political, national crises, defense, legislative, ceremonial.

The Great thoughts. Compiled by George Seldes, Foreword by Henry Steele Commager. Rev. and updated. New York, Ballantine books, 1996. 543 p. PN6081.G636 1996. "From Abelard to Zula, from ancient Greece to contemporary America, the ideas that have shaped the history of the world."

Lend me your ears: great speeches in history. Selected and introduced by William Safire. 1st ed. New York, Norton, 1992. 957 p. PN6122.L4 1992.

McCants, David A. Patrick Henry, the orator. New York, Greenwood Press, 1990. 172 p. E302.6.H5M37 1990.

The Modern presidency and crisis rhetoric. Edited by Amis Kiewe. Westport, Conn., Praeger, 1994. 246 p. JK518.M64 1994. Looks at presidential discourse with examples from several administrations.

Oratory in the Old South, 1828-1860. Prepared under the auspices of the Speech Association of America. Edited by Waldo W. Braden. Baton Rouge, Louisiana State University Press, 1970. 311 p. PS407.07.

Peterson, Houston. A treasury of the world's great speeches. Each speech prefaced with its dramatic and biographical setting and placed in its full historical perspective. New York, Simon and Schuster, 1965. 866 p. PN6121.P4 1965.

Representative American speeches, 1991-1992. Edited by Owen Peterson. New York, H.W. Wilson Co., 1992. 216 p. LRS92-14449. Seventeen speeches on current events and issues.

The Rhetoric of struggle: public address by African American women. Edited by Robbie Jean Walker. New York, Garland, 1992. 445 p. PS663.N4R47 1992. Text of speeches.

Short, Brant. The rhetoric of the post-Presidency: Herbert Hoover's campaign against the New Deal, 1934-1936. Presidential studies quarterly, v. 21, spring 1991: 333-350. LRS91-3699. "In evaluating Hoover's campaign against the New Deal, this case study will examine the rhetorical dimensions of the post-presidency in American political debate."

Smith, Craig Alien. Smith, Kathy B. The White House speaks: presidential leadership as persuasion. Westport, Conn., Praeger, 1994. 263 p. JK518.S583 1994. "This book takes Richard Neustadt's dictum that presidential power is the power to persuade and Jeffrey Tulis's description of The Rhetorical Presidency seriously enough to argue that we can profitably study presidential leadership rhetorically."

Speeches of the American presidents. Edited by Janet Podell and Steven Anzovin. New York, H.W. Wilson Co., 1988. 820 p. J81.C88 1988.

Springen, Donald K. William Jennings Bryan: orator of small-town America. New York, Greenwood Press, 1991. 194 p. (Great American orators, 0898-8277; no. 11) E664.B87S67 1991.

Talbott, Frederick. Churchill on courage: timeless wisdom for persevering. Nashville, Tenn. Thomas Nelson Publishers, 1996. 1 v (unpaged). DA566.9C5 T25 1996.

Vallin, Marlene Boyd. Mark Twain: protagonist for the popular culture. Westport, Conn., Greenwood Press, 1992. 184 p. PS1338.V35 1993. After the Civil War, Americans witnessed an age known for its "silver-tongued oratory", Mark Twain was such a nineteenth-century speaker. Includes speeches.

Voices of multicultural America: notable speeches delivered by African, Asian, Hispanic, and Native Americans, 1790-1995. Deborah G. Straub, editor. New York, Gale Research, 1996. 1372 p. PS663.M55 V64 1996.

Waggenspack, Beth Marie. The search for self-sovereignty: the oratory of Elizabeth Cady Stanton. New York, Greenwood Press, 1989, 204 p. (Great American orators, 0898-8277; no.4) HQ1426.W33 1989. Women orators.

Wisdom of the great chiefs: the classic speeches of Red Jacket, Chief Joseph, and Chief Seattle. Collected and with introductions by Kent Nerburn. San Rafael, Calif., New World Library, 1994. E98.07W57 1994. Indian orators.

Women public speakers in the United States, 1925-1993: a bio-critical sourcebook. Edited by Karlyn Kohrs Campbell. Westport, Conn., Greenwood Press, 1994. 491 p. HQ1412.W68 1994. Includes quotations by famous American women.

Directories of Quotations and Humor

The Athena treasury: 101 inspiring quotations by women. Edited by Marty Maskall. Fair Oaks, Calif., Attitude Works Pub. Co., 1993. 111 p. PN6081.5.A84 1993.

Bartlett, John. Familiar quotations: passages, phrases, and proverbs traced to their sources [online] (as of Dec. 6, 1996). Available Internet: http://www.cc.columbia.edu/acis/bartleby/bartlett/. LRS96-7949. Copyright 1995-1996. Older quotations to 1871. Reference material on the Internet.

——— . Familiar quotations: a collection of passages, phrases, and proverbs traced to their sources in ancient and modern literature. Boston, Little, Brown, 1992. 1405 p. PN6081.B27 1992.

Blakely, James "Doc" How the platform professionals keep'em laughin'. Houston, Tex., Rich Pub. Co., 1987. 294 p. PN4121.H587 1987. How to develop and present a humorous speech. Over 2000 jokes and stories.

Bushisms. Compiled by Jonathan Bines, Andrew Sullivan and Jacob Weisberg. New York, N.Y., Workman Pub., 1992. 87 p. E838.5.B872 1992.

Cohen, J.M. The Penguin dictionary of twentieth-century quotations. London; New York, Penguin Books, 1995. 628 p. PN6081.C548 1995.

Famous Black quotations. Edited, selected, and compiled by Janet Cheatham Bell. New York, Warner Books, 1995. PN6081.3.F36 1995.

Hatlen, Theodore W. You're on!: a speaker's handbook plus one thousand quips and jokes. Santa Barbara, Calif., Dorcas Press, 1993. 292 p. PN4193.I5H38 1993.

Humes, James C. More podium humor: using wit and humor in every speech you make. New York, HarperPerennial, 1993. 244 p. PN4193.I5H79 1993.

Humorous quotations. Compiled by Des MacHale. Cork: Mercier Press, 1994. 221 p. PN6084.H8 H8 1994. Short section of political quotations.

Letterman, David. David Letterman's new book of top ten lists and wedding dress patterns for the husky bride. New York, Bantam Books, 1996. 160 p. PN6162.L378 1996.

Margolis, Jon. The quotable Bob Dole: witty, wise, and otherwise. New York, Avon Books, 1996. 154 p. E840.8D64 A25 1996.

McFadyean, Melanie. Thatcher's reign: a bad case of the blues. London, Chatto & Windus, 1984. 128 p. DA591.T47M43 1984.

The Merriam-Webster dictionary of quotations. Springfield, Mass., Merriam-Webster, 1992. 501 p. PN6081.M494 1992.

Native wisdom. Edited by Joseph Bruchac. San Francisco, HarperSanFrancisco, 1995. E98.P5N383 1995. Indian quotations.

Mr. Kaplan, tear down this wall: Bartlett's missing quotations. Policy review, no. 66, fall 1993: 4-19. LRS93-8872. Objects to the apparent omission of quotations by Ronald Reagan and other conservatives in the new 16th edition of Bartlett's Familiar Quotations, edited by Justin Kaplan. "Policy Review here offers a sampling of conservative quotations from the past 50 years that ought to be considered for Bartlett's 17th."

Powell, Colin L. In his own words. 1st ed. New York, Berkley Pub. Group, 1995. E840.5.P68 A25 1995. May not be in LC.

Prochnow, Hebert Victor. Speaker's and toastmaster's handbook. Rocklin, Calif., Prima Pub., 1992. 357 p. PN4193.I5P717 1992.

Respectfully quoted: a dictionary of quotations requested from the Congressional Research Service. Washington, Library of Congress, for sale by the Supt. of Docs., G.P.O., 1992. 520 p. PN601.R435.992. The 2100 quotations in this book are drawn from the Quotation File created and maintained by the Congressional Reference Division for use in the Congressional Reading Room of the Library of Congress. Covering a variety of subjects of interest to Members of Congress, they include quotation citations that have been requested over and over again. Copies of this book are kept in all congressional reference centers.

Strupp, Jim. Revolution song: Thomas Jefferson's legacy. Summit, N.J., Ashland Press, 1992. 126 p. E332.2.S86 1992.

Sunbeams: a book of quotations. Edited by Sy Safransky. Berkeley, Calif., North Atlantic Books, 1990. 159 p. PN6081.S78 1990.

Wilstach, Frank Jenners. A dictionary of similes. Detroit, Omnigraphics, 1990. 578 p. PN6084.S5W5 1990.

Winokur, Jon. Friendly advice. New York, Plume, 1992. 300 p. PN6083.W56 1992.

The Wit & wisdom of politics. Collected, compiled, and arranged by Charles Henning. Golden, Colo., Fulcrum, 1992. 306 p. PN6288.P6W57 1992.

CRS Prepared Info Packs for Holiday Speechgiving

Speech material: Abraham Lincoln's and George Washington's birthdays; info pack. Updated as needed. IP373A.

Speech material: Fourth of July; info pack. Updated as needed. IP377F.

Speech material: graduation; info pack. Updated as needed. IP379S.

Speech material: Labor Day; info pack. Updated as needed. IP374L.

Speech material: Martin Luther King's Birthday; info pack. Updated as needed. IP372M.

Speech material: Memorial Day; info pack. Updated as needed. IP376M.

Speech material: Thanksgiving Day; info pack. Updated as needed. IP381T.

Chapter 2

SPEECHWRITING IN PERSPECTIVE: A BRIEF GUIDE TO EFFECTIVE AND PERSUASIVE COMMUNICATION

Thomas H. Neale

INTRODUCTION

This chapter reviews various techniques for the research and preparation of effective draft statements by congressional staff for Senators and Representatives.

Writing for the spoken word is a special discipline; it requires that speechwriters' products be written primarily, although not exclusively, to be heard, not read. Speeches are better cast in simple, direct, and often short sentences that can be easily understood be listeners. Rhetorical devices such as repetition, variation, cadence, and balance are available to, and should be used by, the speechwriter.

It is important for speechwriters to analyze audiences according to factors such as age; gender; culture; profession and income level; size of audience; political affiliation, if any; and the occasion for, and purpose of, the speech. Most effective speeches do not exceed 20 minutes in length.

After researching a topic, speechwriters should prepare an outline from which the speech will be developed. They should strive to maintain a clear theme throughout the speech. Most speeches will have a three-part structure consisting of an introduction, a body, and a conclusion.

The accepted style of contemporary American public address is natural, direct, low key, casual, and conversational. This puts listeners at ease and promotes a sense of community between audience and speaker.

Punctuation should reflect the sound structure of the speech, reinforcing the rhythm and pace of actual speech. Clarity of expression is as important a consideration in speech grammar as rigid adherence to rules for written language.

This chapter presents the essentials for speechwriters. Effective delivery can greatly improve a speech. Congressional speechwriters should make every effort to become familiar with the speaking style of the Member for whom they are writing, and adjust their drafts accordingly.

"Rhetoric," wrote Aristotle, "is the power of determining in a particular case what are the available means of persuasion." This report reviews some effective means for the rhetoric of persuasive communication in speeches written by congressional staff for Senators and Representatives. By speeches, this report means draft statements prepared for oral delivery by Members. Such speeches are often prepared under the pressure of deadlines that leave minimal time for extensive revision. Moreover, they must often be drafted in whole or part for Members who may have little opportunity to edit and amend them. The burdens of public office (as well as of campaigning) and the insistent demand for speeches of every kind for a variety of occasions require some degree of reliance on speechwriters, a reliance that is heightened by the limitations of time and the urgencies of the media.

A speech thus "ghostwritten" should nevertheless reflect the intention and even the style of the speaker. The best ghostwriters are properly invisible; they subordinate themselves to the speaker in such a way that the final product is effectively personalized in the process of actual communication. The only ways to achieve or even approach this ideal are practice and experience. This chapter seeks to provide some guidance for congressional staff on the principles and practice of speechwriting. The suggestions offered herein, when combined with practice, attention to audience and occasion, and, most importantly, the Member's attitudes, convictions, and style, can help create a speech that can be a "seamless garment" when delivered by the Member.

This chapter revises and expands an earlier paper of the same title prepared by Charles H. Whittier, Specialist in Religion and Public Policy, former Government Division.

WRITING FOR THE SPOKEN WORD: THE DISTINCTIVE TASK OF THE SPEECHWRITER

Writing effective speeches requires a constant awareness of the distinction between the written and the spoken word: the speechwriter must learn to "write aloud." While the best speeches read as well as they sound, the novice speechwriter should give priority to the ear and not the eye. His or her speech must be written to be heard, not read.

This means that easy intelligibility should be a paramount concern, so that the listening span is not strained. One of the first rules of the speechwriting profession is that a sentence written to be heard should be simple, direct, and short. When the speechwriter "writes aloud," George Orwell's advice to cut out any word that can possibly be cut is helpful, so long as the resulting effect is clarity, and not verbal shorthand.[1] Ciceronian oratory on the one hand and Dick-and-Jane simplicity on the other are extremes to be avoided. The speechwriter thus faces the challenge of crafting words that convey the speaker's meaning clearly, but that also draw on the rich nuance and texture of spoken English.

The average spoken sentence runs from eight to 16 words; anything longer is considered more difficult for listeners to follow by ear, and according to one expert, may be too long for the average listener to absorb and analyze quickly.[2] By comparison, written sentences of up to 30 words are easily understood by average readers.[3] Given these generally accepted limitations, what devices are available to the writer to make more complex sentences and speech wording accessible to the listener? Complex sentences can be clarified by repeating key words and using simple connections. By numerous rhetorical techniques, the speaker states, restates, and states again in different ways, the central themes of the speech.

Repetition and Variation

Repetition with variation is a basic speechwriting tool used by many of the greatest speakers to emphasize key elements while avoiding monotony. Some examples follow.

---

[1] George Orwell, "Politics and the English Language," in *Shooting an Elephant and Other Essays* (New York: Harcourt Brace, 1950).
[2] Edward Bernays, quoted in Mary G. Gotschall, "The Lost Art of Speechmaking," *Campaigns and Elections*, vol. 14, June-July, 1993, p. 48.
[3] William E. Wiethoff, *Writing the Speech* (Greenwood, IN: Alistair Press, 1994), p. 15.

- Martin Luther King's "I have a dream" speech was a striking example of this technique, using that phrase to introduce a series of his visions for a better future.

- Lincoln at Gettysburg emphasized the significance of the day's events by restating the solemnity of the occasion in not fewer than three variations: "We cannot dedicate, we cannot consecrate, we cannot hallow this ground... ."

- Similarly, Winston Churchill's World War II speeches used repetition with variation to build a powerful climax: "We shall fight in France and on the seas and oceans, we shall fight with growing confidence and growing strength in the air. We shall defend our island whatever the cost may be; we shall fight on the beaches and landing grounds, in fields, in streets and on the hills, ...we shall never surrender."

- Franklin D. Roosevelt's 1937 "One third of a Nation" speech imparted a sense of urgency by his deliberate repetition of a "here are" construction to describe conditions in the country, followed again and again with "now":

    - Here is one-third of a nation ill-nourished, ill-clad, ill-housed – Now.
    - Here are thousands upon thousands of farmers wondering whether next year's prices will meet their mortgage interest – Now.
    - Here are thousands upon thousands of men and women laboring for long hours in factories for inadequate pay – Now.

Cadence and Balance

Another venerable rhetorical device is the use of cadence and balance in the spoken word. This is a part of speechwriting where the speaker and the writer need cooperation to ensure success. The tradition of public speaking in the English language owes much to the poetic tradition, which was originally an oral tradition. As one observer noted, "the language of the speech should also be *poetic* — replete with alliteration, metaphor, and other figures of speech. Such adornments, far from being superfluous, enhance meaning and emphasize relationships among ideas."[4] As difficult to define as to achieve, cadence and balance impart a flowing movement and harmonious effect to any speech. Essentially a matter of ordering groups of words (and ideas) into rhythmic patterns, cadence and balance can be attained by such classical rhetorical devices as the ones described below. Do not be put off by the classic Greek names of some of these rhetorical devices; in practice we use them naturally in conversation and writing every day.

Rhythmic Triads

The grouping of words into patterns of three can lead to a memorable effect, provided the device is not overused. Some notable examples from classic oratory include "*Veni, vidi, vici*"; "Never... was so much owed by so many to so few"; "The kingdom, the power, and the glory... "; "I have not sought, I do not seek, I repudiate the support of... "; "one third of a nation ill-clad, ill-nourished, ill-housed... ."

Parallelism

The linkage of similar words or ideas in a balanced construction that repeatedly uses the same grammatical form to convey parallel or coordinated ideas: "Bigotry has no head and cannot think; no heart and cannot feel"; "Charity beareth all things, believeth all things, hopeth all things, endureth all things."

Alliteration

The repetition of initial sounds in a series of words to give emphasis. For instance, "We need to return to that old-fashioned notion of competition — where substance, not subsidies, determines the winner," or, "...the nattering nabobs of negativism... ."

Anaphora

This is the repetition of the same word or words at the beginning of successive clauses or sentences. Churchill's famous defiance of Hitler, "We shall fight on the beaches, we shall fight on the landing grounds... ," which has been previously cited, is one of the most famous examples.

Antithesis

A common form of parallel structure comparing and contrasting dissimilar elements. For instance, "...give me liberty, or give me death.";

---

[4] Judith Humphrey, "Writing Professional Speeches," *Vital Speeches of the Day*, vol. 54, Mar. 15, 1988, p. 343.

"Ask not what your country can do for you — ask what you can do for your country."; "To some generations much is given; from others, much is demanded... "; "A great empire and little minds go ill together."; "It was the best of times, it was the worst of times. It was the age of wisdom, it was the age of folly."; "If Puritanism was not the godfather to Capitalism, then it was godson."

Sentence Variation

This technique involves more than alternating longer sentences with short ones. The writer may employ either periodic sentences, that is, those in which the main clause comes at the end, or loose sentences, in which the main clause is presented at or near the beginning, to be followed by other main or subordinate clauses. Sentence variation also includes the use of such devices as those described below.

Rhetorical Questions

"Is peace a rash system?" "Is life so dear or peace so sweet as to be purchased at the price of chains and slavery?" The speaker leads the audience to the conclusion he hopes they will draw by asking a question that makes his point, and that he intends to answer himself, either immediately, with a flourish, or at greater length during his remarks, through patient exposition.

Sentence Fragments

"Dear money. Lower credit. Less enterprise in business and manufacture. A reduced home demand. Therefore, reduced output to meet it." The speaker dramatizes the situation by reducing it to a stark declaration, which he renders more striking by pausing to let the facts sink in after each sentence fragment.

Inverted Order

"With what dignity and courage they perished in that day." This classic rhetorical practice, once more widely used, seeks to embellish the general flow of words, much like an ornament or a musical flourish. It also helps give a particular sentence special emphasis by causing it to stand out from others by its unusual form.

Suspension for Climax

With this device, the speaker comes to a complete stop in his remarks, using the ensuing moment of silence to concentrate the listeners' attention on his next phrase. "My obligation as President is historic; it is clear; yes, it is inescapable." Even periodic sentences, if used with care, repeating the "suspended" subject or verb before modifying phrases or clauses can contribute to the effect: "Thus did he prove to be a leader who — victorious in battle, magnanimous in victory, skilled in the arts of peace — was able, in the face of his most determined foes... ."

Use of Conjunctions

Repeating key words and using simple connective conjunctions (*and, for, because, but*) can make many complex sentences more easily intelligible to the ear by breaking them up into "bite size" segments. For instance, "Be a craftsmen in speech that thou mayest be strong, *for* the strength of one is the tongue, *and* speech is mightier than all fighting."

Imagery

No speech will sound fresh and vivid if it is not animated by imaginative imagery, by metaphor in its many forms: "the hatred of entrenched greed"; "America will always stand for liberty"; "Democracy is the healthful lifeblood which circulates through the veins and arteries of society... "; "Whether in chains or in laurels, liberty knows nothing but victories."

Extended metaphors or analogies, comparing similarities in different things, should be used with care so that the principal subject will not be lost in the image. Two or more metaphors in a single sentence or thought can be safely ventured only by the most experienced writers — "To take arms against a sea of troubles" — without incurring ridicule (as in the famous — and perhaps apocryphal — example attributed to the newspaper *Pravda*, the onetime propaganda organ of the Soviet Communist Party: "The fascist octopus has sung its swan-song").

Above all, in the spoken word there must be an element of identity and rapport with the listener, whether the speaker uses a "natural" conversational tone or a more oratorical style. Effective speechwriting for Congress is not a branch of "creative writing." Its "rules" are meant to foster clarity of expression, whatever the occasion and purpose of any given speech. Mere clarity is not enough for persuasive rhetoric, however. Indeed, there are times when clarity, brevity, and the like are not appropriate. The issues, because of their import and complexity, may preclude such treatment; similarly, the gravity or delicate political nature of the occasion may call for some measure of deliberate ambiguity. The best speechwriter will take into account the context of the speech and the speaker's personality, the image that is projected — that is, the speaker whom the audience sees and hears. The section on speech analysis in this report attempts a closer look at Lincoln's great Farewell Address at Springfield, illustrating many of the principles considered in this chapter.

AUDIENCE ANALYSIS

What Jefferson Bates called "audience analysis" is probably the single most important factor to be considered in writing every speech: know your listeners, and you will have a much better chance of connecting with them.[5]

Demographics

Bates and others list a number of criteria useful in audience analysis, including, among others: age; gender; culture; education, profession, and income level; size of the audience; and affiliation.[6] Age is obviously an important factor, high school students, young parents, and senior citizens have different levels of life experience, different interests reflecting the challenges they face at their particular stages of life, and, to some extent, they even speak different languages. Although gender differences in societal roles are less pronounced than a generation ago, some believe that certain persistent disparities of viewpoint between many men and women on some topics persist. With respect to "culture," William Wiethoff, in *Writing the Speech,* states that it "has escaped a standard or preferred definition. Speechwriters, however, may envision culture as the race, customs, and religion shared by members of an audience."[7] The factors of education, profession, and income level can be a pitfall for the unwary speechwriter. Never confuse education with intelligence, or professional status and worldly success with moral superiority or virtue, or modest means and educational attainment with the opposite.

---

[5] Jefferson Bates, *Writing with Precision* (Washington: Acropolis Books, 1985), pp. 82-85.

[6] Wiethoff, *Writing the Speech*, p. 22.

[7] *Ibid.*, p. 23.

The writer must be sensitive to these varying frames of reference found in an audience. Draft remarks should be familiar, sympathetic, and topical, without being condescending. They must, as always, be phrased in a way that is natural for the Member, it is painfully obvious to an audience if a Member is not comfortable in his role or with his words.

Audience Size

The size of an audience is another important factor in preparing a speech. A large audience and a formal occasion usually call for greater formality in language and delivery, lengthier remarks, and greater reliance on some of the classical rhetorical practices cited in this report. By comparison, many Members will require only talking points for a town meeting, and will almost certainly speak extemporaneously in still more intimate gatherings. In the age of community cable television and satellite hookups, the Member is often asked to address what may appear to be a very small group of listeners physically present at the broadcast venue; at the same time, however, many others, perhaps thousands, may be viewing from other locations, or from their homes. It is the writer's task to craft remarks that simultaneously take into consideration the people physically present in the studio or location, and those who may be watching from home or other locations.

Degree of Political Affiliation

Speechwriters must also condition their words to the degree of political affiliation, or lack thereof, in the intended audience. A gathering of the party faithful is usually ready for some "red meat." An audience consisting of a non-partisan citizen's group, such as the League of Women Voters, is almost certainly not. The writer must also always remember that, while the Member is affiliated with one political party, and comes from a particular part of the state or district, he or she represents all the people, and gives due attention and respect to the legitimate views and aspirations of all constituents.

OCCASION AND PURPOSE

Another of the speechwriter's tasks is to assess the occasion at which the Member has been asked to speak and tailor the remarks accordingly. In contemporary society, the delivery of remarks by public figures is an expected element in almost every secular public ceremony, and at many religious services. The speechwriter must ensure that the occasion and the speech agree with one another, in both tone and content.

For instance, Veterans' Day and Memorial Day are among the most solemn public holidays in the calendar. For these two events, the speechwriter should focus on themes of commemoration, service, and sacrifice. The atmosphere should appropriately be both somber, and hopeful: "their sacrifice led to a better, more secure life for those who followed them." High school and college commencements are of a different genre altogether. The occasion may demand inspirational remarks, but as one observer noted, "I've heard speakers... deliver a tedious, solemn policy address at graduation ceremonies in which the graduates and families just want to hit the exits and have a good time."[8] Conversely, a formal address to a learned society will differ dramatically from friendly remarks at a neighborhood picnic, town meeting, or retirement home. Simply put, the writer should exercise common sense in preparing remarks appropriate in tone and content to both the audience and the occasion.

Another useful consideration for congressional staff is to plan the delivery of substantive remarks on substantive occasions. If the Member is scheduled to announce a major policy statement or initiative, it should be delivered in commensurate surroundings, and on occasions when media coverage will be adequate. Timing is also a serious factor; speeches delivered at mid-morning, at lunchtime, or early afternoon at the latest, are far more likely to be covered that same day by local TV news.

The purpose of a speech and the occasion at which it will be delivered are closely related. Most frequently, the latter will govern the former. William E. Wiethoff suggests a "purpose" template for speechwriters in *Writing the Speech*.[9] In it he establishes three categories of purpose: *information, persuasion, and entertainment*.

---

[8] Robert A. Rackleff "The Art of Speechwriting," *Vital Speeches of the Day*, vol. 54, Mar. 1, 1988, p. 311.
[9] Wiethoff, *Writing the Speech*, pp. 34-42.

Information

These speeches seek to convey facts or information to the audience. The speaker first identifies the information that is about to be presented, seeking to link the new facts with others the listeners may already be aware of. Next, the speaker elaborates on the details of the information just conveyed, while avoiding a level of complexity and detail that would confuse the audience. Finally, the speaker draws together the facts and ideas related earlier, ideally recapitulating the main points in order to fix them in the listener's memory.

Persuasion

The persuasive speech is a two-edged sword: it can seek to instill in the listeners either the acceptance of, or at least a more favorable opinion toward, a particular condition, fact, or concept. This variant is described as *advocacy*. Conversely, a speech may also attempt to change an audience's impressions, opinions, or most ambitiously, their convictions. Wiethoff calls this *dissent*, and asserts that it is more difficult than advocacy, since the speaker faces the burden of proving to the listeners that what they have heretofore accepted should be modified or rejected.[10] In both cases, the writer must marshal the arguments that will convince the audience.

Entertainment

Wiethoff's third category of speech purpose is entertainment. A great percentage, perhaps a majority, of Member speeches will fall into this category. The choice of title for this group may be misleading, however. These are not necessarily frivolous occasions, and they are not unimportant to the life and people of a town or village, students at a school, or members of a club who constitute the audience for such remarks. Speeches in this category serve the vital function of reinforcing the common ties and experiences that bind communities together and help reinforce the vitality of civic life in America. As Wiethoff notes:

> These speeches are delivered during ceremonies or rituals that are significant in themselves. They do not need clarification in order to be understood. They do not need proof of their importance. Instead, on these

---

[10] *Ibid.*, p. 39.

occasions people share an expectation of what will happen, and they are dissatisfied if the events do not take place as expected.[11]

"Entertainment" speeches may be solemn in nature, such as a Memorial Day address, or celebratory, such as remarks at the opening of a new school, library, or child-care facility. They remind citizens of their joint identity as members of a community; these events, seemingly everyday, or even trite, are actually vital expressions of civic life. The Member's role as a community leader and spokesperson on these occasions should not be underestimated; it is a great honor for him or her to deliver remarks at these community rites, and a congressional speechwriter should devote talent and originality to them.

Obviously, the three purpose categories cited here are not necessarily mutually exclusive; in order to convince an audience, a speaker often needs to combine persuasion with information. Similarly, while some types of remarks are intended purely for entertainment, such as a celebrity roast, the careful speechwriter will always seek to entertain audiences in order to capture and retain their attention.

TIME AND LENGTH

How long should a Member speak? The answer to this fundamental question of speechwriting, like so many others, depends on a wide range of factors. Audience analysis and occasion have been previously noted, but the habits and attitudes of the speaker must also be taken into consideration.

The natural inclinations of the Member must be examined. Is the Member a person of few words, or is he or she a good talker? Does the Member stick to the text, or lay it aside to share anecdotes, personal reminiscences, or even humor, with the audience? These and other related questions can be answered only through experience on the part of the congressional speechwriter. Learning the Member's style and preferences will result in a better product that communicates more effectively.

Time of Day

Time of day should be considered by the writer. In the morning, people are relatively fresh, and are generally better prepared physically to listen

---
[11] *Ibid.*

attentively. By late afternoon, or after a luncheon, however, the audience may need to be stimulated, either by coffee or by lively remarks. Finally, lengthy after-dinner remarks should almost never be inflicted, especially on a paying audience. The potential auditors are full, tired, and ready to go home. It's best to give them their wish as quickly as possible.

How Many Words?

Finally comes the classic question: how many words should the speechwriter prepare? Once again, the factors of audience, occasion, Member preference, and time of day should be considered. The question of length of time, however, must be dealt with at some point. A number of classic speech authorities suggest that in most cases 20 minutes should be the upward limit. Conventional wisdom often holds that most listeners tune out, perceptibly or not, after that period.[12] Ritual or *pro forma* speeches, such as occasional remarks at schools, churches, or public functions where the Member is a guest, but not the main attraction, benefit from brevity, perhaps being limited to five to 10 minutes. Although substantive public policy speeches may merit greater length, in modern America, only presidential inaugural and State of the Union messages seem to exceed the 20-minute limit regularly, with the latter often weighing in at over an hour.

The question of pace is also important; is the Member a fast talker? Different speakers exhibit considerable variety in pace, ranging from 115 to 175 words a minute. Once again, the speechwriter will factor these personal differences into his work. As a benchmark, however, an often-cited rule-of-thumb is that the average 20-minute speech contains about 2,600 words, or, about 130 per minute. Most word processing programs will provide a total document word count as part of their spell check feature.[13]

Having a fixed time stimulates careful preparation. Both a time limit and notes or text help guard against *logorrhea*, or excessive verbiage. Time limits also encourage speakers not to be overly comprehensive, saying everything there is to be said on the speech topic. This is a temptation difficult to resist, but a speech is, by nature, a precis or digest. Excessive complexity or verbiage are capable of transforming an effective speech into something ponderous and exhausting. Jefferson's sharp judgment of 1824

---

[12] Kenneth Roman and Joel Raphaelson, *Writing That Works* (New York: Harper and Row, 1981), p. 73.
[13] For instance, in WordPerfect 7.0, click on "File;" select "Document," then "Properties," and then "Information" to obtain a word count.

applies today with equal force: "Amplification is the vice of modern oratory.... Speeches measured by the hour die with the hour."

SPEECH RESEARCH

Theme, audience, time, place, occasion and purpose — once these are settled, the speechwriter's next concern is to gather ideas, facts, examples, illustrations, quotations, and humor, in short, whatever is needed to give substance, character, and interest to the speech. There is no shortcut for researching a speech, although a number of resources can speed the process.

Resources

Apart from legislative and policy resources, there are other basic materials with which every speechwriter should be familiar. These include a good standard dictionary (spell check is not foolproof, and has a rather limited vocabulary). The preferable dictionary is prescriptive as well as descriptive, that is, it prescribes or recommends usage in addition to providing descriptions or definitions. A thesaurus, such as *Roget's*, published in numerous editions since 1852, or J.I. Rodale's *Synonym Finder*, various editions since 1961, is useful in finding the right word and generally superior to the thesaurus feature offered with most word processing programs. For quotations, consult the standard *Bartlett's Familiar Quotations* in any one of its many editions, or *Respectfully Quoted*, a quotation dictionary compiled by the Congressional Research Service. Annual almanacs, such as the *Information Please Almanac* and the *World Almanac*, are often essential for quick reference.

Literary and religious sources include the works of Shakespeare in any readable edition and the English Bible, especially the King James or Authorized Version. Aside from its obvious spiritual aspects, the King James Bible is important for both its literary quality and its tremendous influence on spoken and written English.

Access to some standard encyclopedia, such as *Americana*, or *Britannica*, is also helpful for fact checking and general information. *Chase's Calendar of Events* is a useful annual guide to special observances throughout the nation. A wealth of facts, statistics, and data useful in speech preparation can be found in the annual U.S. Government publication *Statistical Abstract of the United States*, published annually. For sample speeches on many topics of contemporary interest, the speechwriter may wish to consult *Vital Speeches of the Day*, published twice monthly. It provides examples of speeches delivered by recognized public figures on topical questions and major issues and events of the day, and is annually indexed by author and topic. All these sources are available in the La Follette Congressional Reading Room, and most are also available in House and Senate office building reference centers.

Daily newspapers are a familiar, if neglected, resource for speeches; a dedicated speechwriter will read or skim several each day, noting and saving background items that may prove to be useful later. Both national and hometown papers should be included. Other useful sources include weekly news magazines and more specialized journals that cover public policy issues. Here, again, the advent of the World Wide Web provides new sources of information valuable to the congressional speechwriter: home district newspaper web sites may be regularly scanned for local news on issues and events of interest to the Member. These are usually posted on the day they are published, and almost always well in advance of postal delivery of the printed product.

SPEECH PREPARATION

Building Blocks: Suggested Principles

Certain general principles may be useful to guide the congressional speechwriter in choice of content and style:

- Quotations and humorous anecdotes or remarks are like spices, and should be used with discrimination, mindful of good taste and effectiveness. Speeches overloaded with quotations and anecdotes can sink from their own weight.

- Pseudo-quotations should be avoided. Never use a quotation that cannot be verified in an authoritative source.

- Unless a writer is gifted with lightness of touch, self-deprecating or gentle humor is usually more effective than satire or ridicule.

- Jokes aimed at people's personal lives or at religious and ethnic groups are invariably offensive, regardless of the speaker's motives. Avoid them.

- Statistics should be used with care and moderation. Like the points in an outline, they are better alluded to in context than cited in tedious detail. A speech filled with statistics becomes a statistical abstract, not a speech.

- When selecting material, the responsible speechwriter will take great care to quote accurately and give full credit for whatever is borrowed outright. *Plagiarism is often illegal and always unethical.* On the other hand, it is entirely proper to *adapt* existing materials to one's own purpose in preparing a new speech for any occasion. As Thomas Jefferson wrote in response to accusations that he had plagiarized parts of the Declaration of Independence from other works, "I did not consider it as any part of my charge to invent new ideas altogether and to offer no sentiment which had ever been expressed before." Straining after originality, which has been defined by an anonymous wit as "imitation not yet detected," can ruin the best of speeches.

- Finally, the seasoned speechwriter soon learns to recycle the best parts of previous efforts, to save time and effort, and also to preserve a particularly fine turn of phrase.

The Speech Outline

The task of actually writing the speech, once the preliminaries are completed, will be greatly facilitated in most cases by the use of an outline. The novice speechwriter may be tempted to dispense with this device, on the grounds that it adds a time consuming extra step to a process that is often constrained by tight deadlines. On the other hand, it forces the writer to plan and organize his thoughts, to determine in advance what he intends to say, and to begin at the beginning.

A speech outline generally is not nearly as detailed as an outline for an academic work, such as a journal article, or even a research paper. The outline serves as a skeleton, a framework to carry the flesh and blood of the fully developed speech. At the same time, this skeleton should eventually be invisible, clothed in delivery with ideas and emotions, and as simple as possible; beware of explicitly enumerating too many points or topics. Outlines may be written in topics, or key sentences, or in complete thoughts, so long as there is an orderly sequence.

The frugal writer will retain speech outlines, since they can easily be reworked for future efforts. In whole or in parts, these can be placed in folders in a word processing program, or written out into a looseleaf notebook binder or even on index cards. From any of these media, the outlines can be quickly cut, rearranged, or added to as future occasions may require. President Ronald Reagan, for example, was legendary for his expert use and reuse of note cards that included facts and themes he sought to emphasize in various speeches.

Thematic Clarity

Throughout the speech, the writer ought to be constantly asking: "What is it I am trying to say?" and, after it is written: "Have I, in fact, said it clearly, succinctly, and well?" Every speech seeks in some way to move an audience, to win support, to motivate, to convince, perhaps to inspire, or simply to entertain. Adhere to the central theme or idea while addressing it in different ways, much in the manner that good sentences are constructed for a paragraph.

The arrangement of ideas and themes should follow a logical progression. Each fact establishes a certain point, which leads to the speaker's next point, and so forth, ultimately climaxing with the thematic conclusion. While it is more dramatic to gain an audience's attention by opening a speech with a grand conclusion, be sure that the initial dramatic assertion is followed up by the essential process of weaving the argument the Member seeks to make.

Do not try to say too much, particularly when the speech is intended as the vehicle for a major announcement or initiative. The most memorable presidential inaugural addresses have been those that set a single theme, or coherent group of related themes.[14] Stick to no more than three major points, rather than attempting to say a little something about everything. Anything more risks running afoul of Churchill's famous comment concerning a bland dessert: "This pudding has no theme."

---

[14] For a selection of presidential inaugural addresses, see: Jefferson's first, 1801; Lincoln's second, 1865; Roosevelt's first, 1933; Kennedy, 1961; and Reagan's first, 1981. These and all others are available online at the CRS Home Page at (http://www.loc./ gov/crs). Click on the "Congressional Staff Reference Desk" icon, and select "Speech Writing."

Structure

Three-Part Structure

Nearly every speech will have a basic three-part structure of introduction, body, and conclusion. An arresting introduction should lead into an emphatic statement of the main theme or themes. The argument that follows seeks to elaborate and develop the theme convincingly and effectively — that is, without too much detail. The central theme is restated in the closing peroration. One helpful approach for overcoming the feeling of word fright (what can I say and how?) is to write the speech in reverse: begin with the conclusion, which should summarize the central message, while abridging and restating whatever goes before. If the introduction sets the tone and establishes initial appeal or rapport, the closing communicates the final effect and is more likely to be remembered. Working backward is one way of imparting unity, coherence, and emphasis to the speech as a whole.

Techniques of Persuasion

There are many techniques available for the actual writing of a speech. Almost all speeches delivered by, or on behalf of, Members of Congress, even those for ceremonial or *pro forma* occasions, will have a certain political character because of the Member's representative function, and also because of the way in which his or her office is perceived. In the rhetorical context, political means persuasive, including the expression of personal interest and concern, assuring and reassuring, conveying the Member's identity with each audience, and so creating a community of interest and trust. Three kinds of persuasive techniques are usually distinguished:

- the appeal to reasonableness: "Surely Democrats and Republicans alike can agree that there is no excuse today for hunger in the world's richest nation... ."

- the appeal to emotion: "Can we, as a nation, close our eyes to the spectacle of millions of children going to bed hungry every night...?"

- the ethical appeal (that is, to the character of the audience): "our historic traditions of decency and generosity demand that we face squarely the question of hunger in America... ."

All three approaches may be used in any given speech.

Attention-Problem-Solution

One popular option for developing a speech is the "attention-problem-solution" method, especially for longer speeches of a non-partisan character. Useful for many different occasions, this method begins by stimulating the interest of the audience, usually with attention-grabbing examples of a problem that needs to be recognized and confronted. The speaker then moves to define the "problem" situation, and concludes with the proposed "best" solution, presented so as to win listener support.

This or Nothing

Another option, the "this-or-nothing" method, advocates a policy mainly by presenting and refuting proposed alternatives as inadequate or worse. It lends itself well to partisan occasions or to stirring those already convinced. In every case the speaker seeks to reinforce and strengthen his principal ideas as they are unfolded in the speech. Prior audience analysis and subject preparation will often help the speech "write itself."

No speaker should ever apologize for his or her presence, or for the content of the speech. If it truly deserves apologies, it is better left unsaid. Further, a prudent speaker, rightly wary of the impulse to speak "off-the-cuff," will make certain that "extemporaneous" or "impromptu" remarks are not unprepared. For most speakers it is also better not to memorize a speech (unless one has a gift for it), since memory is fallible and elusive at best.

Style

The congressional speechwriter should not shrink from commonly accepted contemporary usage: the all-day speeches and obscure classical allusions of Daniel Webster and Henry Clay make wonderful reading, but they are history. The development of public address systems, radio, and, finally, the "cool" medium of television, have combined with other social changes to turn down the volume, both in decibels and emotions, of public speaking in the United States, for better or worse eliminating its more histrionic qualities.

Contemporary Style and Tone

The accepted style of contemporary oratory is generally low key, casual without being offensively familiar, and delivered directly to the audience in a conversational tone and volume. It puts the audience at ease and helps promote psychological bonding between listeners and speaker. The speaker is perceived as a neighbor or friend, as well as an elected official. This is, of course, what every Senator and Representative strives to be. Perhaps the first, and certainly one of the most effective, practitioners of this art was President Franklin Delano Roosevelt, in his radio "fireside chats." His calm, reassuring voice and homey language revolutionized the bond of communication between the American people and their Presidents. It could be said that FDR spoke "with," rather than "to," the people, a standard to which Members can honestly aspire today. Once again, certain exceptions are allowed, but these are generally reserved largely to the President, or for only the most formal occasions.

Use natural words and phrases in a speech; let the sentences flow conversationally. It is helpful for some writers, time permitting, to prepare a first draft hi longhand, shaping the sentences slowly, speaking aloud the phrases they intend to use.

The first person is perfectly acceptable in modern public discourse, and when combined with other personal pronouns — remember to avoid "I" strain — it can help connect listener to speaker and create a sense of community within the audience. While the first person singular is sometimes deprecated, it is its *excessive* use that should be avoided. Conversely, speakers should avoid referring to themselves in the first person plural (we) or the third person singular (he or she). The former has been reserved to monarchs, and is considered archaic in modern speech. The latter too often conveys a sense of excessive self importance to listeners. For instance, a Member should think twice before referring to himself or herself in the third person singular: "Dave (or Mary) Smith thinks the problem of hunger is the greatest challenge facing America today."

Writers should generally use simple, declarative sentences, preferably in active voice, when making important statements of fact, assertion, or opinion. Use of the passive voice should not be dismissed out of hand, however; it is sometimes the more desirable form, and can lend grace and variety to the speaker's flow of words that stimulates the listener. It is excessive use that should be avoided. Similarly, exclusive use of the active voice can impart a choppy, juvenile cadence to even a content-rich speech.

Pitfalls to be Avoided

Just as there are points to emphasize in every speech, serving as clear transitions or aural signposts for paragraphs ("secondly," "nevertheless," "finally," "accordingly," "as a result," "in spite of," "as I have said," etc.), so there are things to avoid, and they are more numerous. While they are discussed in full in many reference works, they include:

- jargon and trendy neologisms: "interface," "impact" used as a verb, "parameters," *et al.*;

- redundancy resulting from excess verbiage, not deliberate restatement;

- mannerisms that may distract the listener, and trite phrases or cliches, with the exception previously mentioned, monotony of style or pace, and, in general, language inappropriate to the audience and occasion.

Punctuation

Punctuation is crucial to an effective speech; it helps to clarify the delivery of the spoken word. Good punctuation in English, apart from a few basic elements, is less a matter of inflexible rules than of purpose and style, particularly where speeches are concerned. Historically there have been two broad traditions of punctuation: syntactical — that is, guided by syntax or grammatical construction; and elocutionary — deriving from the rhythm and pace of actual speech. One writer has further distinguished three methods of punctuating:

- by structure or logic to indicate the sense of what is being said;

- by the rhythm of word order and intended meaning — a subtle use best avoided by novice speech writers;

- and by respiration — that is, by the physical ease of natural speech, which assumes that what is read is really spoken.[15]

This last method, essentially the same as the elocutionary style, is the most widely used and certainly the most appropriate for speeches. In short, punctuate according to the ear and not the eye. This also means punctuating for the lungs: give the Member time to breathe! A long and convoluted sentence (something to be avoided in general) can leave the Member literally gasping for breath as he or she concludes it. A useful practice for congressional speechwriters is to declaim aloud (speak aloud, not in a conversational tone, but as if one were speaking to an audience) any lengthy

---

[15] Herbert Read, *English Prose Style* (New York: Pantheon, 1980), pp. 33-51.

sentence intended for the Member. If the writer finds it taxing on the lungs, then so will the Member; in such cases, it is advisable either to fashion shorter sentences, or to repunctuate the original, using such obvious "time out" devices as the colon and semi-colon, both of which are described in the next paragraph.

Commas and dashes are useful to the speaker and listeners alike as guideposts to what lies ahead in a speech. They also provide pauses where the speaker can let the import of the previous sentence sink in, or simply catch his or her breath. Opinion is divided on colons and semicolons; some consider them as serving the same functions as commas and dashes, while others suggest that they are more emphatic, demanding a full stop in the flow of remarks, rather than a short pause. They are also sometimes criticized as leading to long compound sentences that are difficult for audiences to process, and that are better replaced by shorter declarative ones. In the final analysis, the Member's personal preferences and style should be the congressional speechwriter's guide.

Grammar and Syntax

Correct grammar and syntax in the context of speechwriting and delivery mean using a level of English usage that is appropriate to the occasion. While it is highly desirable, the formal grammar of the written language is not an end in itself; it exists to further the clarity of expression. Far more important than the grammarian's rules is the communication of personality by which a speech, as opposed to a lecture, is clothed with emotion and enthusiasm, so that the speaker is perceived to be sincere and trustworthy, neither "talking over people's heads" nor "talking down" to them. While this may belong more to the presentation or delivery, the writer should strive for it in speech preparation as well.

SPEECH PRESENTATION

Effective delivery can transform a weak speech and make it sound very good. Poor delivery can ruin the best-prepared speeches, and sometimes does. Although delivery is not the concern of the speechwriter as such, it must be always in mind as a speech is actually written. The speaker's pace, his or her style, mannerisms, tendencies (such as departing from a text), peculiarities, or special difficulties (words to avoid) — these are elements with which the writer should be well acquainted before preparing any speech. Knowing how a Member speaks is essential in preparing a draft that is both useful and realistic.

Ideally, a speech draft ought to be reviewed three times — by the writer, by the prospective speaker, and by a disinterested third party. Of these three, priority should ordinarily be given to the speaker. The revised product is likely to be more effective. However, with speeches, as with food, too many cooks are undesirable. Moreover, time seldom permits this much critical evaluation and rewriting. It may even be easier to provide for some appraisal of the speech's impact and audience reaction after delivery. For example, it is said that Senator Robert F. Kennedy's speech writers would follow his delivery of a speech word by word, noting those phrases or ideas that were well received, or others that created problems.

An effective political speech is defined not by rules of rhetoric, but by the character of response it evokes. The speaker, then, is always concerned to measure that response and to elicit "positive feedback." This means a network of contacts that can report on the opinions and reactions of the audience, and evaluate the interest generated and evident a week or more after the event. It requires an awareness of media coverage and subsequent treatment from constituents, the sponsoring organization, and others. In short, it means adding a political relevance to the familiar phrase, "keeping in touch."

Although there are substantial distinctions between legislative and non-legislative speeches, the basic principles of preparation and presentation are identical for both. Good writing is nurtured by wide reading, which in turn fosters a sense of style, enriched vocabulary, accuracy in grammar, and a feeling for English syntax. The best speechwriters will, through regular daily reading, bring an ever more abundant background to their work. Everything is grist for the speechwriter's mill. Moreover, nothing is surer in speechwriting than that "practice makes perfect." The more one writes, the easier the task becomes, and the smoother and more conversational the flow of the Member's remarks.

As with so many aspects of speechwriting and delivery, the physical form of a speech is a matter of personal preference. Some speakers prefer to work from a completely polished text, one that may include carefully tailored "spontaneous" anecdotes and jokes at appropriate places, and may even incorporate hints on speech delivery or effective body language in the text. Others prefer to speak from notes derived from such a text, proceed from a series of "talking points," or simply extemporize. Whichever method is used, preparatory notes or an outline are recommended, with the cautionary warning that dependence on a manuscript can deaden the delivery, just as the excessive use of notes or cards can stimulate verbosity.

ANALYSIS OF LINCOLN'S FAREWELL TO HIS NEIGHBORS

President-elect Lincoln's farewell speech at Springfield, Illinois on February 11, 1861 is arguably the shortest great speech ever delivered from the back of a train. Its railway car setting recalls to mind the now-vanished connection between political events and the railroad, including the whistle-stop campaigns of most presidential candidates from William Jennings Bryan to Dwight Eisenhower. What Jacques Barzun called Lincoln's "workaday style [would become] the American style par excellence," undermining the monopoly exercised by purveyors of "literary plush."[16] The Springfield speech illustrates with extraordinary brevity — it is only a 15 line paragraph — the Lincolnian qualities of precision, vernacular ease, rhythmic virtuosity, and elegance.

The sense of right order and emphasis throughout culminates in the closing sentence — "one of the greatest cadences in English speech."[17] The effect is achieved by the simple yet artful devices of parallelism, the balancing of similar and antithetical words phrases, and ideas, evoking rich Biblical overtones among his hearers. Lincoln's style is rooted in the "speaking intonations" and "humanly simple vernacular" of everyday speech, heightened by form and rhythm, the distinctively American tradition seen at its best in such writers as Emerson and Frost.[18] Although some hold that today there is no place for rhetorical eloquence, arguing that "bluntness and clarity" and simplistic thoughts are the norm,[19] others assert that the craft of speechmaking, the impact of skilled political rhetoric is as significant as ever in our history.[20] Lincoln's mastery of that craft remains a formidable example.

---

[16] Jacques Barzun, *On Writing, Editing, and Publishing* (Chicago: U. of Chicago Press, 1972), pp. 57, 73.
[17] *Ibid.*, p. 73.
[18] Richard Poirier, *Robert Frost* (New York: Oxford U. Press, 1977), p. 13.
[19] Edward N. Costikyan, *How to Win Votes: The Politics of 1980* (New York: Harcourt, Brace, Jovanovich, 1980), pp. 120-122.
[20] Jeff Greenfield, *Playing to Win* (New York: Simon and Schuster, 1980), pp. 109-130.

My Friends: No one, not in my situation, can appreciate my feeling of sadness at this parting. To this place, and the kindness of these people, I owe everything. Here I have lived a quarter of a century, and have passed from a young to an old man. Here my children have been born, and one is buried. I now leave, not knowing when or whether ever I may return, with a task before me greater than that which rested upon Washington. Without the assistance of that Divine Being who ever attended him, I cannot succeed. With that assistance, I cannot fail. Trusting in Him who can go with me, and remain with you, and be everywhere for good, let us confidently hope that all will yet be well. To His care commending you, as I hope in your prayers you will commend me, I bid you an affectionate farewell.[21]

GENERAL OBSERVATIONS AND SUMMARY

The rise and, indeed, the virtual triumph in American political speaking of "the popular conversational idiom," with its emphasis on simplicity, brevity, and terseness, has tended to encourage "simplistic language together with slogans or catch words... ," influenced perhaps by the techniques of mass media advertising and particularly television.[22] "Repetition and retention of a few simple ideas are stressed more than a complex concept."[23] In consequence, some have noted a growing trend toward what some have characterized as a numbing mediocrity: "Since the 1920s more political speakers have addressed larger audiences on a wider range of topics than at any time in history. Yet so marked is the decline in the quality of style that the majority of speeches are pedestrian, prosaic, and impotent."[24] This last may be an excessively pessimistic evaluation of the state of contemporary political speech. Few, moreover, would advocate a return to the florid style of public speaking that prevailed as recently as the 1920s.

The remedy, in part, may be the cultivation of style. "Time should be devoted," writes L. Patrick Devlin, "to using impressive language," which he defines as "the most vivid, clear, concise, and meaningful style."[25] It will be

---

[21] Abraham Lincoln, "Farewell Address at Springfield, Illinois," in *The Collected Works of Abraham Lincoln*, vol. IV, Roy P. Basler, ed. (New Brunswick, NJ: Rutgers U. Press, 1953), pp. 190-191.
[22] James L. Golden, "Political Speaking Since the 1920s," in *Contemporary American Speeches*, Will A. Linkugel, R.R. Allen, and Richard L. Johannesen, eds., 2nd ed. (Belmont, CA: Wadsworth Pub Co., 1969), p. 170.
[23] L. Patrick Devlin, *Contemporary Political Speaking* (Belmont, CA: Wadsworth Pub. Co., 1971), p. 14.
[24] Golden, *Contemporary American Speeches*, p. 178.
[25] Devlin, *Contemporary Political Speaking*, p. 14.

most effective if it bears the personal stamp of the speaker. "The process of persuasion is... more a matter of communicating values than logical information."[26] In essence, good speechwriting requires that the speaker assume a role: to some extent, he or she must be able to impart confidence and to sense the character of an audience. We need not agree with Talleyrand's cynical observation that "speech was given to man to disguise his thoughts" to recognize that effective persuasion calls for the ability to win the hearts and minds of listeners. To seem natural is not easy; as George Fluharty and Harold Ross wrote in *Public Speaking*.

> "The speaker is estimating his audience and his audience is estimating him. His ethics, his integrity, understanding, and humanity are strong forces for good and also strong components of his "ethos" or personal effect upon not only his present but also his future audiences. The speaker should therefore make sure that the actual situation permits him to use a given persuasive device.[27]

Once again, the words of Abraham Lincoln, himself no mean practitioner of the public speaker's art, may serve to summarize the speechwriter's ultimate goal:

> When the conduct of men is designed to be influenced, persuasion, kind, unassuming persuasion, should ever be adopted. It is an old and true maxim that "a drop of honey catches more flies than a gallon of gall." So with men. If you would win a man to your cause, first convince him that you are his sincere friend. Therein is a drop of honey that catches his heart, which, say what he will, is the great high-road to his reason, and which, when once gained, you will find but little trouble convincing his judgment of the justice of your cause, if indeed that cause really is a good one.[28]

---

[26] James H. McBath and Walter R. Fisher, "Persuasion in Presidential Campaign Communication," *Quarterly Journal of Speech*, vol. 55, Feb. 1969, p. 18.
[27] George W. Fluharty and Harold R. Ross, *Public Speaking* (New York: Barnes and Noble, 1981), p. 276.
[28] Address before the Washingtonian Temperance Society of Springfield, IL, Feb. 22, 1842. Quoted in Caroline Thomas Harnsberger, *The Lincoln Treasury* (Chicago: Wilcox and Follett, 1950), p. 43.

INDEX

A

active voice, 30
advocacy, 21
alliteration, 14, 15
American public address, 12
Americana, 24
analogies, 17
anecdotes, 22, 25, 33
anthologies of quotations, vii, 1
antithesis, 15
antithetical words phrases, 34
appeal to emotion, 28
appeal to reasonableness, 28
Aristotle, 12
artful devices, 34
assertion, 30
attention to audience and occasion, 12
attention, 5, 12, 17, 19, 22, 27, 29
attitudes, 12, 22
audience analysis, 18
audience(s), 2, 6, 11, 12, 16, 18-24, 27-33, 35, 36
aural signposts, 30

B

balance, 11, 14
balanced construction, 15

Bartlett's Familiar Quotations, 9, 24
basic materials, 24
body, 12, 28, 33
brevity, 17, 23, 34, 35
Britannica, 24
Bryan, William Jennings, 8, 34

C

cadence, 11, 14, 30
catch words, 35
celebrity roast, 22
ceremonies, 20, 21
Chase's Calendar of Events, 24
churches, 23
Churchill, Winston, 8, 14, 15, 27
Ciceronian oratory, 13
citizens, 18, 22
civic life, 21, 22
clarity of expression, 12
clarity, 13, 17, 32, 34
classic Greek names, 15
clear transitions, 30
cliches, 31
closing sentence, 34
coherence, 28
commemoration, 20
common ties, 21
community leader, 22
community rites, 22

complex sentences, 13, 17
conclusion, 12, 16, 28
Congressional speechwriters, 12
constituents, 19, 33
contemporary oratory, 29
content-rich speech, 30
context of the speech, 18
conversational idiom, 35
conversational tone, 17, 29, 31
convictions, 12, 21
creative writing, 17
culture, 8, 11, 18
customs, 18

D

daily newspapers, 25
Declaration of Independence, 26
declarative sentences, 30
deliberate ambiguity, 18
deliberate restatement, 31
delivery, 4, 5, 12, 19, 20, 25, 26, 31-33
Democrats, 28
dictionary, 9, 10, 24
different languages, 18
disinterested third party, 33
dissent, 21
dramatic assertion, 27
dramatic, 7, 27

E

easy intelligibility, 13
education, 18
educational attainment, 18
effective draft statements, 11
Eisenhower, President Dwight, 34
elegance, 34
elocutionary, 31
emphasis, 15, 28, 34, 35
English Bible, 24
English language, 14
English speech, 34

entertainment, 20, 21, 22
ethical appeal, 28
excessive complexity, 23
experiences, 2, 21
exposition, 16

F

facts, 16, 21, 24, 27
familiar phrase, 33
Farewell Address, 18, 35
figures of speech, 14
first person plural, 30
first person, 30
fixed time, 23
flowing movement, 15
formal address, 20
frugal writer, 27

G

ghostwriters, 12
ghostwritten, 12
graduates, 20
grammar, 32, 33
grammatical construction, 31
grammatical form, 15
great speeches, vii, 1, 7
grouping of words, 15

H

harmonious effect, 15
high school and college commencements, 20
high school students, 18
histrionic qualities, 29
holidays, vii, 1, 20
how-to manuals, vii, 1
humor, 9, 22, 24, 25
humorous stories, vii, 1

I

"I have a dream" speech, 14
identity, 17, 28
imagery, 17
Information Please Almanac, 24
information, 20-22, 24, 25, 36
initial sounds, 15
inspirational remarks, 20
intelligence, 18
introduction, 6, 12, 28
inverted order, 16

J

jargon, 31
Jefferson, Thomas, 10, 26
joint identity, 22
jokes, 9, 25, 33

K

Kennedy, Senator Robert F., 33
King James Bible, 24
King, Martin Luther, 10, 14

L

La Follette Congressional Reading Room, 25
legislative and policy resources, 24
length of time, 23
life experience, 18
Lincoln at Gettysburg, 14
Lincoln's farewell speech, 34
Lincolnian qualities, 34
listener support, 29
listeners, 11-13, 17-19, 21, 23, 29, 30, 32, 36
local news, 25
logical progression, 27
logorrhea, 23
loose sentences, 16
looseleaf notebook, 27

M

main clause, 16
major policy statement, 20
mannerisms, 31, 32
mass media, 35
media coverage, 20, 33
members of a community, 22
Memorial Day, 10, 20, 22
metaphor, 14, 17
modern oratory, 24
moment of silence, 17
monotony, 13, 31
moral superiority, 18

N

natural words and phrases, 30
news magazines, 25
newspaper, 17, 25
non-partisan citizen's group, 19
non-partisan, 19, 29
note cards, 27

O

occasion, 11, 14, 17, 19, 20, 22-24, 26, 31, 32
occasional remarks, 23
offensive, 25
"One third of a Nation" speech, 14
oral delivery, 12
oral tradition, 14
oratorical style, 17
Orwell, George, 13
outline, 11, 26, 33
overly comprehensive, 23

P

pace, 23, 31, 32
parallel or coordinated ideas, 15
parallel structure, 15
parallelism, 15

passive voice, 30
periodic sentences, 16, 17
personal preference, 33
personal reminiscences, 22
persuasion, 7, 12, 20, 22, 36
persuasive rhetoric, 17
plagiarism, 26
poetic tradition, 14
polished text, 33
political affiliation, 11, 19
political events, 34
political nature, 18
political party, 19
ponderous and exhausting, 23
positive feedback, 33
practice and experience, 12
precision, 34
presentation of a speech, vii, 1
principal subject, 17
pro forma occasions, 28
pro forma speeches, 23
professional status, 18
prudent speaker, 29
pseudo-quotations, 25
psychological bonding, 29
public address systems, 29
public ceremony, 20
public discourse, 6, 30
public functions, 23
public speaking, 2-4, 14, 29, 35
punctuation, 12, 31
purpose of a speech, 20

R

race, 18
radio, 29, 30
Reagan, President Ronald, 27
redundancy, 31
religion, 18
religious services, 20
repetition, 11, 13-15, 35
Representative(s), 7, 11, 12, 30
Republicans, 28

Respectfully Quoted, 24
revision, 12
rhetoric of persuasive communication, 12
rhetoric, 3, 6, 7, 12, 33, 34
rhetorical devices, 11, 15
rhetorical eloquence, 34
rhetorical questions, 16
rhythm and pace, 12, 31
rhythmic patterns, 15
rhythmic triads, 15
rhythmic virtuosity, 34
rituals, 21
Roget's, 24
Roosevelt, President Franklin Delano, 14, 30
rule-of-thumb, 23

S

schools, 23
seamless garment, 12
secular, 20
self importance, 30
Senator(s), 11, 12, 30
sense of community, 12, 30
sentence fragment(s), 16
sentence variation, 16
Shakespeare, 24
simple connective conjunctions, 17
simplistic language, 35
size of the audience, 18
slogans, 35
societal roles, 18
sound structure, 12
speaker, vii, 1-6, 8, 9, 12-14, 16, 17, 21, 22, 25, 27, 29, 30, 32, 33, 36
speaker's personality, 18
speaking intonations, 34
special emphasis, 16
specific occasions, vii, 1
speech grammar, 12
speech preparation, 25
speech topic, 23

speech wording, 13
speech writers, 31, 33
speechwriter(s), 11-13, 18, 20, 22-26, 29, 31-33, 36
spell check, 23, 24
spoken word, 11, 13, 14, 17, 31
sponsoring organization, 33
stark declaration, 16
Statistical Abstract of the United States, 24
statistics, 24, 26
students, 21
style, 12, 22, 25, 29, 31-35
subordinate clauses, 16
substantive occasions, 20
successive clauses, 15
suspension for climax, 17
Synonym Finder, J.I. Rodale's, 24
syntactical, 31
syntax, 31, 32, 33

T

techniques of persuasion, 28
television, 19, 29, 35
thematic conclusion, 27
themes, 13, 20, 27, 28
thesaurus, 24
third person singular, 30
"this-or-nothing" method, 29
three-part structure, 28
time of day, 22, 23

timing, 20
tone and content, 20
trendy neologisms, 31
trite phrases, 31

U

unity, 28
unusual form, 16

V

variation, 11, 13, 14, 16
verbal shorthand, 13
verbiage, 23, 31
vernacular ease, 34
Veterans' Day, 20
vital expressions, 22
Vital Speeches of the Day, 15, 20, 25
vocabulary, 24, 33

W

Wiethoff, William E., 13, 18, 20, 21
word count, 4, 23
word processing programs, 23, 24
World Almanac, 24
World War II speeches, 14
World Wide Web, 25
worldly success, 18
write aloud, 13